THE FRAGRANCE
OF FRIENDSHIP

Compiled by
ALICE GRAY

Art by
KATIA ANDREEVA

BLUE COTTAGE GIFTS™
a Division of Multnomah Publishers, Inc.
Sisters, Oregon

THE FRAGRANCE OF FRIENDSHIP

©2001 by Blue Cottage Gifts™
Published by Blue Cottage Gifts™ a division of Multnomah Publishers® Inc.
P.O. Box 1720, Sisters, OR 97759

ISBN 1-58860-005-X

Artwork by Katia Andreeva
Artwork designs by Katia are reproduced under license from Koechel Peterson
& Associates, Minneapolis, MN, and may not be reproduced without permission.
For information regarding art featured in this book, please contact:
   Koechel Peterson & Associates
   2600 E. 26th St.
   Minneapolis, MN 55406
   612-721-5017

Designed by Koechel Peterson & Associates, Minneapolis, MN

Multnomah Publishers Inc. has made every effort to trace the ownership of all
poems and quotes. In the event of a question arising from the use of a poem or
quote, we regret any error made and will be pleased to make the necessary
correction in future editions of this book.

Please see the acknowledgments at the back of the book for complete attributions
for this material.

Scripture quotations are taken from *The Living Bible* (TLB) 1971. Used by
permission of Tyndale House Publishers, Inc. All rights reserved, and *Contemporary
English Version* (CEV) © 1995 by American Bible Society.

Printed in China

01 02 03 04 05 06 — 10 9 8 7 6 5 4 3 2 1 0

www.gift-talk.com

CONTENTS

THE FRAGRANCE OF FRIENDSHIP

A friend," someone wrote, "is one who knows the song in your heart—and can sing it back to you when you've forgotten the words."

There is no better gift in all the world than a dear friend who knows you well—and loves you still! Acquaintances come and go, but true friendship is like a pathway through a fragrant summer garden.

What do you find in such a garden? You find dearly loved rosebushes, with blooms that seem to grow more lovely with the passing years. You also find shy, delicate new flowers, opening to the sunlight for the very first time. So it is with friendship. Some friends have graced our lives for years. We have found strength in their stability, comfort in their familiar presence, and we have marveled at the constancy of their love. Other friends have arrived with a new season of life…bright and cheering as the flowers that lift their faces to the sun.

What a delightful garden this is! How soothing to linger through a long afternoon, to talk and laugh and dream…and maybe share a few tears. It is a garden where pretenses are set aside and we can just be who we are…knowing we will be loved all the same.

The stories within this small book may remind you of cherished friends now far away, of loyal friends who have walked with you for years, and of new friends who swirl into your life like a playful breeze. Linger over these pages, friend, and fill your heart with the fragrance.

Happiness comes to those who are fair to others and are always just and good.
-PSALM 106:3, TLB

MORNING WALK

Author unknown • from In The Company of Friends

Six A.M. Two women in windsuits are out for their morning walk. As they walk, they talk about their important friendships: husbands, kids, coworkers. They occasionally touch each other's shoulders, stop, face each other, and laugh. A sun-dried seventy-something man, wearing a neon orange ski hat, walks by, smiles, and says, "You two look like you're doing ballet together." And so they are. As friends, they are dancing in synchrony: listening, encouraging, challenging each other.

Friendship...serves a great host of different purposes all at the same time. In whatever direction you turn, it still remains yours. No barrier can shut it out. It can never be untimely; it can never be in the way. We need friendship all the time, just as much as we need the proverbial prime necessities of life, fire and water.

-CICERO

SAVING THE BEST FOR LAST

Rochelle M. Pennington • from God's Math

aving the best for last." The old cliche crossed my mind as we waited for dessert to be served. Undoubtedly, it would be wonderful; worth the wait.

Tonight was our annual ladies Christmas party, and the evening had been a delight. The meal, preceded by a short program, was followed by a gift exchange.

One by one we stood up to open the present which had been placed on the table before us. Small gifts. Simple gifts. Candles, stationery, bubble bath. Polite applause responded to each.

It was not until this orderly process had made a full circle to the last person remaining that anyone noticed that she didn't have a gift to open…and then everyone noticed at once.

Her name was Dorothy, our older—and newest—

member. Having joined us nearly a year ago after moving to the community, this was her first Christmas party.

An awkward silence fell upon those gathered as we waited for someone to think of something—and to think of it quick—to save Dorothy from embarrassment. And then someone did. It was Dorothy.

Standing up, she reached for her purse and removed a brown paper grocery sack. Unfolding it, she looked inside the seemingly empty bag, then looked at us.

"Let me tell you about my gift," she said. "I received love and kindness and friendship from you. For these, I am grateful. Thank you."

Dorothy sat down to a roar of applause.

And for the second time, the old cliche crossed my mind. The best, again, had indeed been saved for last.

*Nothing makes so much impression on
the heart... as the voice of friendship*
-Rousseau

The glory of friendship is not in the outstretched hand, nor the kindly smile, nor the joy of companionship; it is in the spiritual inspiration that comes to one when he discovers that someone else believes in him and is willing to trust him.

-RALPH WALDO EMERSON

MAY BASKET

Sue Dunigan • from Decision magazine

ey, do you know what? Today is May Day!" my sister announced. "Do you remember the May Day baskets we used to make with colored paper and paste?"

Childhood memories and warm-feelings engulfed me as I recalled that my sisters and I would run around our neighborhood delivering the not-so-perfect baskets brimming with spring flowers. We would place the handmade treasures on a doorstep, knock on the door, then scurry away as fast as our legs could carry us. It was delightful to peer around a bush and watch our friends open their doors and pick up the colorful gift, wondering who had left it out for them.

I distinctly remember the May Day of the year that I was in fifth grade. That year I was faced with a challenge involving one of my dearest friends. She lived right across the road from our family, and we had walked together to school nearly every day since first grade.

Pam was a year older than I, however, and her interests were starting to change from the interests that we had had together. A new family had recently moved into our small town, and Pam was spending more and more time at their house. I felt hurt and left out.

When my mother asked me if I was going to take a May Day basket to Pam's house, I responded angrily, "Absolutely not!" My mom stopped what she was doing, knelt down and held me in her arms. She told me not to worry, that I would have many other friends throughout my lifetime.

"But Pam was my very best friend ever," I cried.

Mom smoothed back my hair, wiped away my tears and told me that circumstances change and people change. She explained that one of the greatest things friends can do is to give each other a chance to grow, to change, and to develop into all God wants them to be. And sometimes, she said, that would mean that friends would choose to spend time with other people.

She went on to say that I needed to forgive Pam for hurting me—and that I could act out that forgiveness by giving her a May Day basket.

It was a hard decision, but I decided to give her a basket. I made an extra-special basket of flowers with lots of yellow because that was Pam's favorite color. I asked my two sisters to help me deliver my basket of forgiveness. As we watched from our hiding place, Pam scooped up the flowers, pressed her face into them, and said loudly enough for us to hear, "Thank you, Susie! I hoped you wouldn't forget me!"

That day I made a decision that changed my life:
I decided to hold my friends tightly in my heart, but
loosely in my expectations of them, allowing them space
to grow and to change — with or without me.

*Forgiveness out to be like a cancelled note —
torn in two, and burned up, so that it never
can be shown against one.*
-HENRY WARD BEECHER

THE HANDS OF FRIENDS

Jane Kirkpatrick • from A Burden Shared

A winter wind whipped past her through the parlor door. Before her, women sat and stitched. Their worn and wrinkled fingers pulled together pieces of her past cut into little squares: a child's worn dress, a bedroom curtain, a flowered tablecloth (with the berry stain her husband made one holiday cut out and now discarded). Dozens of memories they patched together.

That day the women did the final stitching, making perfect edges then tying the tiny strings to keep the stuffing behind each quilted piece. They sewed the

It is threads, hundreds of tiny threads which sew people together through the years.
-SIMONE SIGNORET

single-colored backing down. The comforter, completed, would keep her warm through winter's winds.

What comforts are the memories, the patches that mark the past and then are held together with the stitching hands of friends placed over solid backing. Surrounded by the fondness, we recall the memories, let them nourish us, keep us warm, and give us much needed sleep; knowing in the morning we can set aside the quilt, rested, still wrapped in comfort.

In these difficult days, I give my comforter to you. May the memories you wish to savor wrap themselves around you, stitched together by the hands of friends.

*The greatest gift you can give another
is the purity of your attention.*
-RICHARD MOSS

*A*s dew to the blossom, and bud to the bee,
as the scent to the rose, are those
memories to me.

-AMELIA B. WELBY

TEARDROPS OF HOPE

Nancy Jo Sullivan

My friend Lauri and I had brought out our kids to the park that day to celebrate my 35th birthday. From a picnic table we watched them laugh and leap through the playground while we unpacked a basket bulging with sandwiches and cookies.

We toasted our friendship with bottles of mineral water. It was then that I noticed Lauri's new drop earrings. In the thirteen years I'd known Lauri, she'd always loved drop earrings. I'd seen her wear pair after pair: threaded crystals cast in blue, strands of colored gemstones, beaded pearls in pastel pink.

"There's a reason why I like drop earrings," Lauri told me.

Friendship is one of the sweetest joys of life.
Many might have failed beneath the bitterness
of their trial had they not found a friend.
-CHARLES SPURGEON

She began revealing images of a childhood that changed her forever, a tale of truth and its power to transform.

It was a spring day. Lauri was in sixth grade, and her classroom was cheerfully decorated. Yellow May Day baskets hung suspended on clotheslines above desks, caged hamsters rustled in shredded newspaper and orange marigolds curled over cutoff milk cartons on window shelves.

The teacher, Mrs. Lake, stood in front of the class, her auburn hair flipping onto her shoulders like Jackie Kennedy's, her kind, blue eyes sparkling. But it was her drop earrings that Lauri noticed most—golden teardrop strands laced with ivory pearls. "Even from my back-row seat," Lauri recalled, "I could see those earrings gleaming in the sunlight from the windows."

Mrs. Lake reminded the class it was the day set aside for end-of-the-year conferences. Both parents and students would participate in these important progress reports. On the blackboard, an alphabetical schedule assigned twenty minutes for each family.

Lauri's name was at the end of the list. But it didn't matter much. Despite at least one reminder letter mailed home and the phone calls her teacher had made, Lauri knew her parents would not be coming.

Lauri's father was an alcoholic, and that year his drinking had escalated. Many nights Lauri would fall asleep hearing the loud, slurred voice of her father, her mother's sobs, slamming doors, pictures rattling on the wall.

The previous Christmas Lauri and her sister had saved baby-sitting money to buy their dad a shoeshine kit. They had wrapped the gift with red-and-green paper and trimmed it with a gold ribbon curled into a bow. When they gave it to him on Christmas Eve, Lauri watched in stunned silence as he threw it across the living room, breaking it into three pieces.

Now Lauri watched all day long as each child was

escorted to the door leading into the hallway, where parents would greet their sons or daughters with proud smiles, pats on the back and sometimes even hugs. The door would close, and Lauri would try to distract herself with her assignments. But she couldn't help hearing the muffled voices as parents asked questions, children giggled nervously and Mrs. Lake spoke. Lauri imagined how it might feel to have her parents greet her at the door.

When at last everyone else's name had been called, Mrs. Lake opened the door and motioned for Lauri. Silently Lauri slipped out into the hallway and sat down on a folding chair. Across from the chair was a desk covered with student files and projects. Curiously she watched as Mrs. Lake looked through the files and smiled.

Embarrassed that her parents had not come, Lauri folded her hands and looked down at the linoleum. Moving her desk chair next to the downcast little girl,

Mrs. Lake lifted Lauri's chin so she could make eye contact. "First of all," the teacher began, "I want you to know how much I love you."

Lauri lifted her eyes. In Mrs. Lake's face she saw things she'd rarely seen: compassion, empathy, tenderness.

"Second," the teacher continued, "you need to know it is not your fault that your parents are not here today."

Again Lauri looked into Mrs. Lake's face. No one had ever talked to her like this. No one.

"Third," she went on, "you deserve a conference whether your parents are here or not. You deserve to hear how well you are doing and how wonderful I think you are."

In the following minutes, Mrs. Lake held a conference just for Lauri. She showed Lauri her grades. She scanned Lauri's papers and projects, praising her efforts and affirming her strengths. She had even saved a stack of watercolors Lauri had painted.

Lauri didn't know exactly when, but at some point in that conference she heard the voice of hope in her heart. And somewhere a transformation started.

As tears welled in Lauri's eyes, Mrs. Lake's face became misty and hazy—except for her drop earrings of golden curls and ivory pearls. What were once irritating intruders in oyster shells had been transformed into things of beauty.

It was then that Lauri realized, for the first time in her life, that she was lovable.

As we sat together in a comfortable silence, I thought of all the times Lauri had worn the drop earrings of truth for me.

I, too, had grown up with an alcoholic father, and

for years I had buried my childhood stories. But Lauri had met me in a symbolic hallway of empathy. There she helped me see that the shimmering jewel of self-worth is a gift from God that everyone deserves. She showed me that even adulthood is not too late to don the dazzling diamonds of newfound self-esteem.

Just then the kids ran up and flopped onto the grass to dramatize their hunger. For the rest of the afternoon we wiped spilled milk, praised off-balance somersaults and glided down slides much too small for us.

But in the midst of it all, Lauri handed me a small box, a birthday gift wrapped in red floral paper trimmed with a gold bow.

I opened it. Inside was a pair of drop earrings.

A Prayer for Grace

Dale Evans Rogers • from Time Out, Ladies!

ord, thou knowest better than I know myself, that I am growing older, and will someday be old.

Keep me from getting talkative, and particularly from the fatal habit of thinking I must say something on every subject and on every occasion.

Release me from the craving to try and straighten out everybody's affairs.

Keep my mind free from the recital of endless details—give me wings to get to the point.

I ask for grace enough to listen to the tales of others' pains. Help me endure them with patience.

But seal my lips on my own aches and pains. They are increasing, and my love of rehearsing them is becoming sweeter as the years go by.

I dare not ask for improved memory, but for a growing humility and a lessening cocksureness when my memory seems to clash with the memories of others.

Teach me the glorious lesson that occasionally I may be mistaken.

Keep me reasonably sweet. I do not want to be a saint—some of them are so hard to live with—but a sour old woman (or man) is one of the crowning works of the devil.

Make me thoughtful, but not moody; helpful, but not bossy.

With my vast store of wisdom, it seems a pity not to use it; but thou knowest, Lord, I want a few friends at the end.

Give me the ability to see good things in unexpected places, and talents in unexpected people. And give me, Lord, the grace to tell them so.

And since I have no gold to give,
And love alone must make amends
My only prayer is, while I live —

God make me worthy
of my friends.

-Frank Dempster Sherman

Legacy of a Friend

A friend will strengthen you with her prayers,

bless you with her love,

and encourage you with her heart.

-Author unknown

THE CRAZY QUILT

Melody Carlson • from Patchwork of Love

I have an old quilt made by my father's grandmother. It's not a beautiful quilt, and all the fabric appears to be quite old. But I love it.

The pieces are probably leftover scraps from Aunt Fran's apron, little Mary's Easter dress, or Grampa's favorite shirt. They are odd shapes and sizes. Some nameless shapes have hooks and curves, long slivers of fabric painstakingly sewn with dozens of meticulous stitches. A few tiny patches are smaller than my thumbnail.

Some of the fabric is very plain with dull color. I can just hear some tired mother say, "But, dear, it's a very serviceable cloth," while her daughter frowns at the new school dress. Other pieces are bright and cheery, like snippets of birthdays, summer vacations, and fun times gone by. A few fancier pieces are satiny smooth with embossing or embroidery; they seem to whisper of weddings, dances, a first kiss.

My father's grandmother was nearly blind and perhaps that explains why the shades appear haphazardly arranged and almost seem to shout at each other. I wonder if she ever realized what her creations looked like, or did she simply go by touch? They do have an interesting texture—smooth next to bumpy, seersucker alongside velvet; and all over the quilt hundreds of tiny stitches, almost invisible to the eye, pucker ever so slightly.

If I were blind, I would like to make quilts like this.

Recently my own family relocated to a new town, and I was in bed with the flu, wrapped in my great-grandmother's crazy quilt. I felt sorry for myself and I missed the friends I'd left behind. Deep down, I knew it was partly my own fault—I hadn't taken steps to establish new friendships. Several acquaintances seemed willing, but I was holding back, hesitating.

As I studied the crazy quilt, I thought of the many friends I'd had throughout my life. Some felt a bit scratchy and rough like a sturdy piece of wool, but in time they softened—or I became used to them. Others were delicate like silk and needed to be handled with care. Some were colorful and bright and great fun to be with. A few special others felt soft and cozy like flannel, and they knew how to make me feel better.

Many of my friends have only been around for a season. So often I've had to leave them behind, or they leave me! And yet, in my heart, I know they are friends for life. If I met them on the street tomorrow, we would hug and laugh and talk nonstop. It would seem like yesterday.

And that's because God has sewn them into my heart.

I pulled the old quilt closer around me, comforted and warmed by my memories. Surely, my own masterpiece—this quilt of friendships I fretted over—was not nearly finished, I would make new friends in this town. And like my great-grandmother, trusting her fingers to lead her, I would, by faith, reach out.

It is my joy in life to find

At every turning of the road,

The strong arm of a comrade kind

To help me onward with my load.

And since I have no gold to give,

And love alone must make amends

My only prayer is, while I live—

God make me worthy of my friends.

-FRANK DEMPSTER SHERMAN

Happiness comes to
those who are fair to others and
are always just and good.

-Psalm 106:3, TLB

CHANCE MEETING

Jane Kirkpatrick • from A Burden Shared

They shared a neighborhood and street, these friends, shared good memories, good times. When each wife became a widow within weeks of the other, they shared in mourning, too. The women made a pact that no hour would be too late to wake the other when the memories and loss became so great that only a friend's embrace could get them through. No need to call ahead, just knock on the other's door. Each agreed to give in this special way.

One night the grief became so great it woke her, the anguish so real it sliced through her troubled sleep.

In her night dress, she fled into the darkness seeking solace at her neighbor's door. She did not make it. Instead, she met her friend midstreet, equally seeking, reaching for the comfort found only inside understanding arms.

A friend is one who stands to share
Your every touch of grief and care.
He comes by chance, but stays by choice;
Your praises he is quick to voice.
No grievous fault or passing whim
Can make an enemy of him.
And though your need be great or small,
His strength is yours through it all.
No matter where your path may turn
Your welfare is his chief concern.
No matter what your dream may be
He prays your triumph soon to see

-EDGAR A. GUEST

I WANT THAT ONE

Charles Stanley • from How to Keep Your Kids on Your Team

I heard a story once about a farmer who had some puppies for sale. He made a sign advertising the pups and nailed it to a post on the edge of his yard. As he was nailing the sign to the post, he felt a tug on his overalls. He looked down to see a little boy with a big grin and something in his hand.

"Mister," he said, "I want to buy one of your puppies."

"Well," said the farmer, "these puppies come from fine parents and cost a good deal."

The boy dropped his head for a moment, then looked back up at the farmer and said, "I've got thirty-nine cents. Is that enough to take a look?"

"Sure," said the farmer, and with that he whistled and called out, "Dolly. Here, Dolly." Out from the doghouse and down the ramp ran Dolly followed by four little balls of fur. The little boy's eyes danced with delight.

Then out from the doghouse peeked another little ball; this one noticeably smaller. Down the ramp it slid and began hobbling in an unrewarded attempt to catch up with the others. The pup was clearly the runt of the litter.

The little boy pressed his face to the fence and cried out, "I want that one," pointing to the runt.

The farmer knelt down and said, "Son, you don't want that puppy. He will never be able to run and play with you the way you would like."

With that the boy reached down and slowly pulled up one leg of his trousers. In doing so he revealed a steel brace running down both sides of his leg attaching itself to a specially made shoe. Looking up at the farmer, he said, "You see, sir, I don't run too well myself, and he will need someone who understands."

Every man rejoices twice when he has a partner of his joy; a friend shares and makes it but a moiety, but he swells my joy and makes it double.

-JEREMY TAYLOR

Uncommon Friendship

Dr. Bettie B. Youngs • from Values from the Heartland

I will help you," the little boy said, reaching for Norma's tiny hand and placing it in his own. "And I won't let anyone laugh at you no more." We watched, awed by his skills of compassion—uncommon, we thought, for one as young as us.

It was the first day of kindergarten. Too shy to ask the teacher to use the bathroom and too timid to use it without first getting permission, five-year-old Norma sat at her small desk crying because she had wet herself.

It wasn't long before all the other students heard her soft whimpers and began staring in her direction. Some

No soul is desolate as long as there is a human being for whom it can feel trust and reverence.
-George Eliot

students laughed because they thought her predicament funny; others giggled, no doubt out of relief that it had happened to her and not to them. But one brave little boy did not laugh. Instead, Norm got up from his desk, walked over to his classmate and looking at her, said softly, "I will help you." We were all sitting and he was standing, so his presence seemed almost majestic. "And I won't let them make fun of you," he said reassuringly.

My tiny classmate looked up at Norm and smiled with admiration. His act of kindness had buffered her duress; she no longer felt afraid and alone. She had found a new friend.

Still holding her small hand, the little hero turned, surveyed his classmates and asked kindly, "How would you feel if it happened to you?" The wise teacher at the head of the classroom observed quietly, but said nothing.

We children sat motionless, stilled partly by the enormous strain and anxiety caused by the drama in this moment, but also because we had just witnessed an act of heroism we had not been able to summon in ourselves. It was a lesson in how precious goodness can be.

Then the little boy added, "Let's not laugh at her anymore, okay?" Intuitively, we knew we were in the presence of courage.

And by his actions, we were persuaded to develop some of our own.

Editor's note: Norma never forgot Norman, nor he her. Their friendship is now celebrating its thirty-sixth year.

If you love someone you will be loyal to him no matter what the cost. You will always believe in him, always expect the best of him, and always stand your ground in defending him.
-1 CORINTHIANS 13:7, TLB

Friendship...the greatest love,

      the greatest usefulness,

      the most open communication,

      the noblest sufferings,

      the severest truth,

      the heartiest counsel,

and the greatest union of minds of which

brave men are capable.

      -JEREMY TAYLOR

BLOSSOMS

Kimber Annie Engstrom

The fragrance of a true friend

Looks for blossoms

While watering the heart.

ACKNOWLEDGMENTS

A diligent search has been made to trace original ownership, and when necessary, permission to reprint has been obtained. If I have overlooked giving proper credit to anyone, please accept my apologies. Should any attribution be found to be incorrect, the publisher welcomes written documentation supporting correction for subsequent printings. For material not in the public domain, grateful acknowledgment is given to the publishers and individuals who have granted permission for use of their material.

Acknowledgments are listed by story title in the order they appear in the book. For permission to reprint any of the stories please request permission from the original source listed below.

"*Saving the Best for Last*" by Rochelle M. Pennington, newspaper columnist and contributing author to *Stories for the Heart*, *Chicken Soup for the Soul*, and *Life's Little Instruction Book*. You may contact her at N1911 Double D Rd., Campbellsport, WI 53010, (902) 533-5880. Used by permission of the author.